Letters Home
1861 – 1865

By Charles and William Schadt
Edited by Stuart Schadt

Bradley Stuart Books
U. S. A.

ISBN 978-0990761037.

Printed in the United States of America.

Second Edition

Cover Image: The Texas Monument at Manassas National Battlefield Park, erected in 2012.

Foreword

These are letters written home during the Civil War by Charles Schadt and his brother William Frederick Schadt. Charles was born in 1838 and was 23 when he enlisted. William was born Sept. 15, 1845, and was 16 when he enlisted. Most of the letters are addressed to Caroline Schadt (born July 19, 1843) their sister. These three children were the only survivors of the family of Carl and Caroline Schaeffer Schadt, who came to Galveston, Texas in 1846 with the Fisher-Miller Colony from Grumbach, Germany aboard the Colchis. Traveling with them from Grumbach was Caroline's sister and brother-in-law the Junkers. The father and mother died of yellow fever in Galveston in 1847. We know with some certainty that the daughter Caroline was raised by the Cranes of Galveston and we believe that they also took in Charles and William. This seems to be confirmed by the frequent references to the Cranes throughout the letters.

Small notes are included in italics with some of the letters to give context to the letters. Wikipedia is often the sited source though other sources and websites are also sited.

As this letter announces Charles and William joined the Lone Star Rifles. This group made up of volunteers from Galveston County was Company L of the 1st Texas Infantry and part of Hood's Texas Brigade. The letter also implies they left without telling their sister of their plan.

Galveston
July 29, 1861

Beloved Sister,

Don't be surprised. William and myself are going to Virginia in the Lone Star Rifles on Thursday the 1st of August. Ere you receive this letter we will be on our route.

Don't grieve about us. You will never have any reason to be ashamed of your brothers, we go there to fight and expect to have enough of it. It is hard to part, but our Country requires us, and as Southern men we must meet the call of our gallant President.

Man for man is the password.

We will go per ship Ruthven to Liberty, thence per rail to Beaumont, from there we have to foot it 110 miles to New Iberia, from there per ship Cricket to Berwick Bay, from there per rail to Virginia. I left my clothes with Mary.

Your affectionate brother,

Charles

Camp Wigfall was later named Camp Carondelet. It is a nationally registered eight acre site adjacent to Cougar Elementary School in Manassas Park, Virginia.

Camp Wigfall, Manassas
Sept. 1, 1861

Dear Sister,

You must excuse me for not writing you any sooner as nothing new of any consequence has transpired since I wrote the few hasty lines in New Orleans.

We arrived here last Sunday and are camped in an apple orchard, have good water and plenty to eat, our tents are very small, 8 by 8 ft., in which 6 have to sleep.

Mr. F.W. Behrman will hand you this letter. I have written him in detail. Ask him to read his letter to you.

William wrote Mrs. Schneider a week ago, which will no doubt be in possession ere this.

As far as health is concerned, I never was so fit and healthy as I am now. I have gained considerable in weight. William is also very healthy and stout and likes the fun which comes with our work. He is on guard this morning over the guard house.

Don't be uneasy about us for we are well taken care of for the present, and as soon as winter comes on we will be put in winter quarters.

I will write again soon. I must now close. The mail wagon is about to start.

Your faithful brother,

Charles

To   Miss C. Schadt
        Galveston

The Tattoo (Mentioned in the next letter.) is a bugle call played in the evening. The original concept of this call was played on the snare drum and was known as "tap-too." Later on, the name was applied to more elaborate military performances, known as military tattoos. The tattoo signals that all light in squad rooms be extinguished and that all loud talking and other disturbances be discontinued within 15 minutes, at which time Taps should follow. Wikipedia Tattoo (Bugle Call)

The Hickory shirt fabric is a relative of denim and as durable as hickory wood. It was a 100 percent cotton tough, soft, classic, all around kind of shirt. It blocked the wind; it easily vented with the buttons; it got sweaty if you did and then it cooled you as the sweat evaporated. They are still available but the inmates in Pendleton, Ore., may be making the last American-made hickory shirts. They can be ordered on line. Source: ForkForum

The Fred this letter is addressed to is the F. W. Behrman charged with delivering the previous letter and the Fred Behrman referred to in the April 29, 1863 letter

Manassas, Sept. 1, 1861

Dear Fred,

I have made up my mind at last to write you a few lines. From our journey from New Orleans here nothing of any consequence, except occasional delays in connection with trains occurred. We arrived here last Sunday and joined the 1st Texas Volunteer Regiment, Col. Wigfall. Our regiment is composed of eleven companies, about 850 men, 10 companies Texas and one Alabama Company.

The health of the regiment is pretty good. There are a few cases of chills and fever and some dysentery, but no measles. There are some regiments here with 2/3rds down with the measles, but they are not fatal. There are but 5 in our company sick: Lt. Bidell, Mr. Early, Nick Nicholson, F. Burke and Wm. Young.

The provisions we receive are very good and comprised of 1-1/4 fresh meat, 1-1/3 flour or cornmeal, coffee, sugar, rice, bacon, mess pork, vinegar, salt and pepper, soap and candles. Enough to eat and plenty of work.

Our rules are Revelle at 5 o'clock a.m., Roll call at 5 ½ a.m., breakfast 6 ½ a.m., company drill from 7 to 9 a.m., Battalion drill from 9 to 12 m., dinner 1 p.m., Battalion drill from 2 to 6 p.m. Dress parade from 6 to 6 ½ p.m., supper 7 p.m., tattoo and roll call 9 p.m., lights and cures out at ½ past nine. Silence in camp. I have to quit. Battalion drill.

On account of it being Sunday today we only drilled til eleven o'clock so we have one leisure hour for our Sunday. Our drill ground is very rugged and hilly. We have to march through woods, over fences, across ditches and gullies, and keep line as soon as on firm ground, or the devil is to pay. Col. Wigfall is very strict in his commands and any negligence of duty is 48 hours extra duty or drill with packed knapsack.

McLeod of Galveston is Major of the Regiment. He is not well liked by the whole regiment, although none have any reason to hate the man, for he acts as a gentleman. It is the old grudge the boys have against him, which will wear way as far as our Company is concerned. We are all satisfied with our officers, especially Capt. McKeen, who acts as a father to the boys and provides for our comfort to his full extent. We are suffering for nothing at present, but will in a very short time, for winter is coming on us and we will be in want of flannel, which you cannot buy for love or money. To give you an idea of the exorbitant prices they charge at Manassas Junction I will give you the prices current: Hickory shirts $2.00, common brogans $2.50, $6.00 woolen socks, no cotton socks. 40 to 50 cts. per Canton flannel drawers, $2.00 whiskey, $3.00 per quart. A regular thieving set of settlers.

We have a fair prospect of a fight in a few days. The pickets are within 2 ½ miles of Alexandria and at Falls Church and are fighting daily, taking prisoners on both sides. Day before yesterday they brought in 15 Yankees. Today we have a report that they have made some of our boys prisoners. We may have to start for Fairfax County at any minute. We received the order 3 days ago to hold ourselves in readiness to strike tents, then the real work will begin. The Confederate Army within 20 miles is estimated at from 180,000 to 200,000 men. The whole county looks like one camp and everything is alive with men. I have seen a great many Texans and also Galvestonians on other Regiments. New ones visit us every day. William is well and satisfied. He is on guard duty today guarding the guard house. He says this is quite different from Galveston street parading and a little more work than fun. I will have to close, so goodbye.

Enclosed please find a few lines addressed to my sister, which please hand to her. Give William's and my respects to Mr. and Mrs. Jenny, Mrs. Schneider, Gus Wakelee, Frank Hitchcock, Von Harten and (*Text Unclear*), and all who enquire for us. I would mention more names but…

So farewell and write often and give me all the news about Galveston, and tell Gus Wakelee to write also.

Yours as ever,

Chas. Schadt

P.S. Our present camp is about 3 ½ miles from the Junction and 5 miles from the late battlefield, 2 miles to Bulls Run. William sends his respects to Louis Dure and should like to see him shoulder a musket alongside of him just for fun.

My address is Private Chas. Schadt, Company L, Capt. McKeen

1st Texas Regiment, Col. Wigfall
Manassas Junction, Va.

Munson's Hill mentioned in the third paragraph is located in the area of Seven Corners in Fairfax County Virginia. Flags flown from the top of the hill could be seen in Washington, D. C. making it strategic in several ways. Source: Munson's Hill Wikipedia. The Wikipedia article on General Rosecrans credits him with victories at Rich Mountain and Corrick's Ford in July 1861 and with preventing Lee from retaking what is now West Virginia, so the defeat referred to by Charles is unclear.

Camp Texas near Dumfries
Prince William Co. Virginia
October 8, 1861

Dear Sister,

This is the fourth letter I have written to you and I have not received any answers or even a letter from anyone since we left New Orleans. We are all well and hearty and in good spirits. Neither William nor I have had the slightest attack of sickness, in fact I have never felt better in my life, the fresh air of the mountains seems to agree with us very well. It is now what we would call in Galveston chilly and cold, but it does not bother us a bit. We are getting gradually used to cold weather and we have not the threat we had a month ago about cold weather, although we are not well prepared with winter clothes. Capt. McKeen tells us that you are preparing winter clothes for us in Galveston. We were very glad to hear it, for you can't buy anything here for love or money.

We are now camped 2 miles from the Potomac, 32 miles below Washington, in the woods, cut off from the main road. We will move in a few days to some better place, where we can drill battalion drills. We have not had any fight as yet, but may have one any day. The largest tramp we had day before yesterday. We marched from 1 p.m. til 10 o'clock that night, about 15 miles towards Fairfax C.H., in search of the Yankees. The Yankees had crossed the Potomac on Occoquan Creek, and landed this side 12 miles above our camp, and destroyed some cornfields and a few uninhabited buildings, among them a church, but on hearing of our approach they recrossed to Maryland. We were joined by about 15,000 men, 24 pieces of artillery and considerable cavalry, all eager for a fight, but all had to return disappointed.

Our troops have evacuated Munson's hill and are falling back to Manassas by degrees. The Yankees are advancing as fast as our troops fall back. There will be the largest battle ever fought yet on this continent in a very short time.

The reason our troops are falling back no one knows except the head Generals, but they know best. It is not fear of being whipped by the Yankees, but for better ground to fight on, is the general supposition. Our force and the Yankees is about equal, say 200,000 near Fairfax. Our battle line is ten miles long and our pickets 40 miles from where we are til up above Centreville.

You have no doubt heard of the battle Lee had with Rosecrans and the defeat of Rosecrans. Also of General

Price's victory in Missouri. It will now be our turn to make a strike.

John Waters requests you to ask his father whether he has not received his letters, and request him to write to him.

We have no sick in our company at present and the regiment is very healthy.

Please give my respects to all who enquire after us.

William and myself send kindest regards to Mrs. Crane and family.

Write me often for I am very anxious to hear from you.

I remain, your affectionate brother,

Chas. Schadt

Address:
Chas. Schadt
Private, Co. L
1st Texas Regt.
Co. Wigfall, Manassas

To Miss C. Schadt
    Galveston

The Civil War In Prince William County *by Jan Townsend, Edited and Expanded by James Burgess gives an account of the October 1861 Potomac River Blockade consistent with what is described by William in this letter but does not name the ships William names. (pp 15 – 17)*

Camp on Potomac, Oct. 19, 1861

Dear Sister,

I have received your welcome favor of the 24th and am very sorry to hear you say that you have not received any letter and I am sure it is not because we did not write, for Charles alone has written you four letters. Since Charles has written you last we have moved and are now camped on Talbot's Hill, which is 900 feet high, 200 yards from the river. Our object is to protect the masked batteries which are on the banks of the river. We have a great deal of excitement here. There are about 150 steamers and 35 sailing vessels lying in the river and dare not pass. Sometimes they try to run the blockade, but do not meet success. Our batteries have just had an engagement between 3 steamers and 2 schooners, of which they sank one steamer and crippled two and captured the two schooners, one of them named Fairfax of New York laden with hay and the other Mary of Washington laden with wood. The Fairfax was struck nine times and the crew had scarce time to save their lives. We have one rifled cannon here called Long Tom, which throws a ball 7 miles and I wish that they had it in Galveston. I hope those large cannons have reached Galveston by this time and I hope they are ready to defend the city. The steamers get very bold sometimes and try to throw shell into our camp. They have done no damage so far. We hear cannonading all day long and expect an engagement between our batteries and the large Yankee fleet which is now lying in the river. I suppose old Abe thinks that the Rebels are a perfect nuisance on the Potomac.

Charles and myself enjoy excellent health and are very well satisfied. Charles sends his best wishes to you and Mrs. Crane and family. Please write to me as soon as possible. I will retire now and go fishing on the Potomac. Please tell Lula that I am 30 miles from the apples now and cannot get any.

I remain your truly brother,

Wm. Schadt

Address
Wm. Schadt
Private, Co. L
1st Texas Regt
Care of Capt. McKeen
Manassas

Camp Quantico, Nov. 27, 1861

Dear Sister,

I have received your letter of the 28th Sept., which I found in the bundle of clothing. I also just received your letter of 7th Nov. which afforded me a great deal of pleasure. I am very much obliged to you and Mrs. Crane for the clothing and blankets which you sent. John Hanson is well and says he will write to Mrs. Harlen and Miss H. King. William Young went to the hospital in Dumfries with the chills and fever about two weeks ago. He is getting along very well now and will come to camp as soon as possible. We are very busy at present. We are fortifying Talbot Hill and erecting another battery towards our left with two large rifled cannon. The Yankees have at each other most every day. One of our gunners was killed the other day by the explosion of a Yankee Shell. Col. Wigfall has been promoted to Brigadier General and his Brigade consists of 1st, 4th, and 5th Texas Regiments, one Louisiana Regiment, and the *(Text unclear)* artillery, containing 8 cannon. McLeod is Col. of our regiment and the boys are very well satisfied with him. The 4th and 5th Texas Regiments are in camp within 5 miles of us and the Bayou City Guards are in the 5th Texas Regiment, and I have had the pleasure of taking dinner with Mr. Ham Settle. I did not see his father or brother. He told me that his father was going back to Texas as soon as possible. For what purpose I don't know. Mr. Waters sends thanks to you for the favor. I will now tell you about our mess. The mess is called the Confederate

Mess, and composed of six members. The following are the names: Chas. Kingsley, John Dillon, John Waters, Ezeck Crawford, Chas. Schadt and Wm. Schadt, and we get along like brothers. We are all splendid cooks and washers, and as soon as we learn how to iron we will be ready for hire out. We don't need a cook, for we can eat all we get without trouble. Tell Mr. Jenny he is very welcome to the pony, and give him my best regards if you see him. I am very proud to say that I have enough clothing to keep me comfortable. Charles has been sick and I have been unwell myself, but we both are all right now. We have plenty of ice and snow. Tell Lula we have no apples, but plenty of snow if she wants any. Charles sends his best respects to Mrs. Crane and family. Please give my best respects to Mrs. Crane and family, too. You must excuse my scribbling for it is so cold that I can hardly hold the pen.

Your affectionate brother,

William Schadt

Camp Wigfall, April 2, 1862

My dear Sister,

I have just received your welcome letter in which you state that Galveston is not to be abandoned, which I am very glad to hear. We left Camp Quantico on the 8th of March and arrived at this camp on the 12th, which is one miles from the City of Fredericksburg on the west bank of the Rappahannock River. The whole army of the Potomac has fallen back in order to make a better stand. The lines which we formerly occupied were 30 miles from any railroad and all provisions had to be transported by wagons. During the winter the roads became so bad that it was impossible for them to bring enough provisions for so large an army and we many a time had to go on half rations, but for all that we were all happy and contented.

Three days after we left our camp the Yankees came over the river in large numbers, but they did not remain any length of time. We have 16 men out scouting from this Regiment. They bring in more Yankees every day. They have already taken 17. A few days ago 5 of our scouts went into their lines and were surrounded by 400 cavalry. Three of them escaped and the other two were tied and carried off. If they kill those two we will kill those 17 for retaliation. When we were in winter quarters Tom Blessing in our company had some deguerrean fixings sent to him and he went to work taking pictures. We have had a picture taken of the mess. Either of them will let you have one to take a copy of if you want it.

The Settle* boys send best respects to you. Mrs. McKeen is in Richmond. She is well. We are very well satisfied with Capt. McKeen. They keep us very strict and drill us hard. I expect we will leave here before long and go into active service. I thank Lula very kindly for the valentine. I am very glad to see young folks with old notions. While writing I received your letter dated March the 12th in which you state that the people feel awful about the enemy getting the upper hand of us. It is very true we have had some very sad reverses lately, but for all that we do not feel uneasy. The only way they have defeated us yet is by taking the advantage of bringing an overpowering army and navy up on us, which we could not resist. We can whip them every day if they come on an equal footing.

I am glad to hear that Texas turns out so many men. Remember me to all my friends. Myself and Charles are both well.

Your affectionate brother,
William

The Settle brothers are mentioned throughout the letters. They are members of the 5th Texas Regiment.

Camp Wigfall
April 6, 1862

Dear Sister,

Since William wrote the above we had another march in pursuit of the Yankees at Stafford Court House, but when we got within 2 miles of them they broke and ran in Bull Run style. We got back here yesterday all well.

Enclose please find a draft on Dr. J.L. McKeen for $10 from me and William. I will soon write you again.

Your truly affectionate brother,
Charles

In haste.

The Battle of West Point is better known as the Battle of Eltham's Landing and is also known as the Battle of Barthamsville. Wikipedia quoting The Official Virginia Civil War Battlefield Guide *reports 194 Union Casualties and 48 Confederate. I am not surprised at the discrepancy in William's numbers and the official numbers. Casualty numbers count both wounded and killed.*

Camp near Richmond
May 17, 1862

Dear Sister,

I take this present and only opportunity I have had to write to you and inform you of the death of dear Brother Charley, who fell gallantly fighting for our glorious cause on the 7th of this month. Dear Sister, I have been so oppressed by grief at the loss of our only and dear brother that I could not nerve myself to write you the intelligence of his death any sooner, but thank God he has nerved me with the spirit of revenge and woe be to the hated Yankee foe that ever I meet. Dear Sister, I pray to God to nerve you in this hour of our affliction and trouble as he is the only one to comfort us in our hardest trials. Dear Sister, do try and pray to God that he may give you courage to stand the blow that has fallen so suddenly upon you, as God is the only one we can put our trust in. He is the only comfort that we can receive. Dear Sister, Charley was decently and respectfully buried. He was laid under a large apple tree and his name and age and also the cause he fell under inscribed upon the tree. Dear Sister, we attacked the enemy and drove them in confusion before us. We killed and wounded 300 and took some prisoners. Our loss was 15 killed and 23 wounded. The loss of our company was Charley and Joe Brown killed and 3 wounded. The fight was near Williamsburg and called the Battle of West Point. Dear Sister, I received your welcome letter by Lieutenant Bedell. Goodbye, dear Sister. I am well and will write soon again. Trust in God and you will be all right.

Your affectionate brother,
William

The Battle of Seven Pines is also known as the Battle of Fair Oaks or Fair Oaks Station. It took place in Henrico County, Virginia. The outcome of the battle was inconclusive with 790 Union soldiers dead and 980 Confederates. General Johnston was wounded in the battle which led to the appointment of Robert E. Lee as Confederate commander. Source: Wikipedia, Battle of Seven Pines.

Camp near Richmond, July 17, 1862

Dear Sister,

I have just received your welcome letter of the 18 of May and hasten to answer. Since the death of dear Brother Charley I have written you four or five letters. In one of them I enclosed 20 dollars which I hope you will receive. I have received no answer to any of them as yet. Dear Sister, I am enjoying good health and hoping to see you before long. Dear Sister, I have been in three battles and thank God I have always come out unhurt. The first was at West Point in which dear Charley was killed, the second was at Seven Pines in which McClellan was badly defeated and compelled to retreat under the cover of his gunboats, where he now remains. The fight lasted six days. We captured a large supply of army stores and provisions, besides 104 cannon and 8,000 prisoners. They left all their sick, dead and wounded in our possession. They burnt a great amount of goods to prevent us from getting them. This last fight has caused a great excitement in the North. The following is a list of the killed and wounded in our company: Poupart killed, Townsend killed, Joseph Nagle wounded in the leg, Sidney Smith wounded in the leg, George Hawkins wounded in the hand, H. Shultz wounded in the arm, Iakoolef wounded in the head. Swarting wounded in the head, Capt. Bedell wounded in the leg and hand, Millard wounded in the arm.

Ham and Charley Settle send kindest regards to you. They are both well. George Delesdenere was killed in the last fight, also Cut Clute. The loss of our regiment is 107 men. Please give my kind regards to Mrs. Crane and family and all those who inquire for me. Please write soon. I remain

Your affectionate brother,

William Schadt

Camp near Richmond July 26, 1862

Dear Sister,

I take this present opportunity to let you know that I am well and hope that these few lines will find you the same. Mr. Chas. Sorley has been in camp and the boys were all glad to see him and hear from home. We have very easy times now. We have nothing to do but drill twice a day and that early in the morning and late in the evening on account of the weather being so hot. It is just as hot here as in Texas. Fruit is plentiful, but no watermelons, which I think are better than all the fruit. We do not expect any fight for some time. There is a great deal of sickness in the Yankee army. Our army is in good health and spirits. The Yankees have got sick and tired of fighting. They begin to see that it is no use to try to conquer the South. The Settle boys are well and send their kind regards to you. Capt. Bedell has recovered from his wounds and is now with the company. All the balance of the wounded are getting along very well. A good many of them have taken furloughs to go to South Carolina and Georgia. Please give my best respects to all the folks. Please write soon.

I remain, your affectionate brother,

William Schadt

I am surprised by Williams brief aside to the Second Battle of Manassas. Aug. 28 – 30, 1862. He obviously thinks Chas. Vidor's account will be sufficient.

Camp near Martinsburg, Va.
Sept. 23 1862

Dear Sister,

I have received your welcome letters of the 6th and 22 of July. I was very glad to hear that you are well. I am in good health and fine spirits and I hope these few lines will find you the same. Since my last letter we have been in two battles, one was fought on the old Manassas battleground and the other at Sharpsburg in Maryland. We went into Maryland and captured several cities and destroyed all the railroad bridges and canals within our reach and then captured Harpers Ferry and 8,000 prisoners and millions of dollars worth of property, besides 5,000 negroes which they had stolen from citizens. In the battle of Manassas our loss was very heavy. We had 3 killed and 18 wounded. List of the killed is as follows: Lieut. J. C. S. Thompson, J. Frank, W. Zimmer. The Settle boys are well. They told me they had a letter from home saying you were well and going back to Galveston. It is no use for me to state the particulars about the fight, for Chas. Vidor has sent a letter giving a full account which will be published.

Dear Sister, please give my best respects to all. Write soon.

Your affectionate brother,
William

The Union forces Occupied Galveston Island, Texas on or about October 8, 1862 according to the American Battlefield Protection Program. They were driven from the Island January 1, 1863.

Camp near Cullpepper, Nov. 12, 1862

My dear Sister,

I take this present opportunity to write you these few lines to let you know that I am well and hoping these few lines will find you the same. I have just received your welcome letter dated Oct. 16 in which you speak about me not getting a furlough. It is not so easy done as you might suppose as they only grant furloughs to those that are sick or wounded. Les Thompson and Mr. Rogers were both sick at Richmond when they got their furloughs and I did not know anything about their going to Texas. You speak about sending me a bundle of clothes for which I will be very thankful to you for the weather is getting very cold. We have had several snow storms. We have just received a suit of winter clothes from the government. I hear that Galveston is in the hands of the Yankees. I hope they will not let them get on the main land. John Delesdenier who got wounded at Manassas has since died of his wounds. All of our boys that were wounded at Sharpsburg and fell into the hands of the Yankees are getting exchanged as fast as they can bear transportation. I hear that John Hanson and Austin Jones are going to Texas on a furlough. We have just received a letter from Capt. Bedell. He was wounded in the cheek and in the shoulder. He is now in Fort Deleware. He says as soon as he gets exchanged he will get a furlough. The boys all say that the Yankees treated them very kindly. Ham and Charley Settle are both well and send their kindest regards. Please give my kind regards to Mrs. Crane and family and all my friends. Write soon.

I remain, your affectionate brother,
William

The Battle of Fredericksburg had the largest concentration of soldiers of any battle during the civil war, 200,000. William identifies the night of the 16th as the date of the Yankee retreat but the official dates are listed as December 11 – 15. The union suffered 1,284 dead, 9,600 wounded. The Confederates suffered 608 dead and 4,116 wounded. It was a resounding defeat for the Union and led to the replacement of General Burnside. Sources: The Battle of Fredericksburg in Wikipedia and in Saving America's Civil War Battlefields, Civil War Trust.

Camp near Fredericksburg
Dec. 18, 1862

Dear Sister,

I take this present opportunity to let you know that I am well and hope these few lines will find you the same. I have received your two letters, one dated Nov. 18 and the other the 1st. I will send this letter by William Young, who is going home on a furlough. We have had a large fight here and whipped the Yankees badly. We repulsed the Yankees nine times with very heavy loss. On the night of the 16 the Yankees recrossed the river where they now remain. Our company did not lose a man. All the boys are well and hearty. The Settle boys are well. Ham is in Richmond and Charley is with his regiment. I have not received that bundle of clothes yet, but I hope I soon will. The weather is very cold and I hope we will go into winter quarters soon. I must close now. It is getting too cold. I will write soon. Give my regards to all.

I remain, your affectionate brother,

William

William uses the term riffle in his letter. The term was unfamiliar to me but with the help Dr. Douglas Wulf PHD I found the following. The Oxford English Dictionary sites its general meaning as to be successful in an attempt or undertaking then sights several uses of riffle in "to make the riffle." It interprets the use as related to the definition of a riffle in a stream as a minor rapid and the meaning to be "to make it through the riffle." Not to argue with the OED but I think it more likely to be related to the meaning of riffle as referring to a style of card shuffling and meaning something like to "make the cut."

Camp near Fredericksburg
Jan. 25, 1863

Dear Sister,

I take this present opportunity to let you know that I am well and hope these few lines will find you the same. I have spent a very merry Christmas and a happy New Year. I hope you have the same. My heart is filled with joy to hear of the return of Galveston. I dare say it was a most brilliant affair. I have not heard any particulars about the fight as yet. I hear that the Island is being well fortified. I hope it is so. I think General Magruder is the right man in the right place. If it is fighting the boys want, he is the man to give it to them. I wish I could have been there and taken a hand in the fight myself. I suppose Wm. Young has reached Texas by this time. Everything is quiet along here. The Yankees are still on the opposite side of the

Rappahannock River. We go on picket once every two weeks. We have plenty of clothes to keep us warm, which is the main thing nowadays. We have not had any orders to go into winter quarters yet, but we have all built ourselves cabins and are now as comfortable as can be expected these times. I tried to get a furlough, but I would not make the riffle. I hope the war will soon be over and we all will get everlasting furloughs. The Settle boys are well. Charley sends his kind regards. Ham is in Richmond at his uncle's. I have not received that bundle of clothes yet. I think they must be lost. Please remember me to all my friends and those who inquire for us. Write soon.

I remain, your most affectionate brother,

William

Camp near Fredericksburg
Feb. 4, 1863

Dear Sister,

I have just received your welcome letters dated Dec. 16
and 25. Jas. Nagle has arrived here and brought the
clothes you spoke about, for which I am under a
thousand obligations to you for them. Everything is
quiet along here. I have just come off picket and
therefore could not sooner write. I spoke to some of the
Yankee pickets. They told me that they were sick and
tired of the war and the expected peace in less than 3
months. I wish it was so. General Burnside, Franklin
and Sumner have resigned. Gen. Hooker is now in
command of the Yankee force. The weather is very cold
and the ground is partly covered with snow. We had a
great game of snow ball a few days ago. There was
about five thousand men engaged in the game. It was a
great sight. Jas. Nagle looks very well, but is not in the
best of spirits, by all appearances his lady love must
have given him the mitten, whoever she is. I don't
know. You ask me who my best friend is. That is very
hard to tell for I have not a single enemy in the
company. The clothes you sent me are a very handsome
Christmas present for me. I wish I had something to
return for them. Jas. Nagle brought us some papers
giving full particulars about the fight at Galveston. The
Settle boys are well. Ham is still in Richmond. I am well
and hearty and hope these few lines will find you the
same. Please give my kind regards to all my friends.

Your affectionate brother,

William

The general consensus of several sites identify Nicarauga Smith as a bad apple. At the beginning of the war he is blamed for a number of small burglaries in Galveston and is banished from the island. He returns and enlists in the confederate army. When the Yankees take Galveston he deserts and joins the Yankees. When the Island is retaken he is captured, tried and executed by military firing Squad. He is said to haunt Galveston's Old City Cemetery. Source: William T. Block website.

Camp near Richmond, March 15, 1863

Dear Sister,

I have just received your welcome letter dated Jan. 6. Leslie Thompson and George Branard have just arrived. Les brought me a letter from you dated Jan. 28 in which I was very glad to hear that you were well. While in winter quarters it was rumored that the Yankees were sending troops on the South side of the James River so Lee sent General Hood's and Pickett's Divisions down here to watch the enemy's movements and check them if they should advance. We left our comfortable quarters on the 17 of Feb. The weather was cold and it was snowing very hard so we had a very hard march of it. We arrived here on the 22 of Feb. and are encamped 7 miles below Richmond on the South side of the James River. Our camp is a very nice one. We have wood and water so handy. Les Thompson looks very well. So does George Branard. A trip home improves the boys very much. Charley and Ham Settle are both in camp and well. I received two pair of socks from you by Ham Settle for which I am thankful to you for them. I am glad to hear that Genl. Magruder is fortifying the Island. I am sure he will not give it up like Genl. Hebert did. I have heard that they hung Nicarauga Smith. I think they did perfectly right, They ought to have hung him 3 years ago. I suppose you have seen Wm. Young before this. He can tell you all the particulars better than I can. I am very well and hope these few lines will find you the same. Please give my kind regards to all my friends. Write soon and I will do the same.

I remain, your affectionate brother,

William

The USS Brooklyn was a union ship stationed off of Galveston Island after the retaking of the Island. She was a sloop-of-war Launched in 1858 and retired in 1889. There is no mention of her during the battle of Galveston. Source: The war of the rebellion: a compilation of the official records of the Union and Confederate armies. ; Series 1 - Volume 15

Camp near Suffolk, Va. April 29, 1863

Dear Sister,

I take this present opportunity to let you know that I am well and hoping these few lines will find you the same. I have just received your welcome letter dated Feb. 15 and was glad to hear that you were well. Dear Sister, while in camp near Richmond I wrote you several letters, but have received no answer as yet. I hope you have received them by this time. We are now encamped within 3 miles of Suffolk which place the Yankees have possession of, and have had for the last twelve months, which gave them ample time to make it impregnable. The city is perfectly surrounded with breastworks and forts. The Nansemond River is on our left, in which the Yankees have 6 gunboats, and the Dismal Swamp is on our right, which is impassable for man or beast. Our artillery had a fight with the gunboats the other day and they sunk one and disabled another. We have had several small skirmishes but did not amount to anything. I do not think that we will attack the enemy in his stronghold but annoy him all we can and try to draw him out. We have been very busy since we have been here. We have to go on picket every two days and remain there thirty six hours. We have now about 800 wagons to work gathering corn flour, bacon and forage. They got at one farm alone 80 thousand pounds of bacon which had been bought by some Yankee government contractor and on hearing of our approach ran off and left it, so it fell into our hands. Leslie Thompson is in the hospital sick. Ham and Charley Settle are both well and send their kind regards.

I understand that Genl. Magruder is going to try and take the Brooklyn. I hope he will succeed. I have not heard from Galveston for a good while and would like to hear from there. I had a letter from Wm. Young in which he says that he had his furlough extended sixty days longer. I have heard of the sudden death of G.A. Behrman. Please let me know what has become of Fred Behrman. I have not heard from him since I left home. Dear Sister, I am well and enjoy good health and thank the Lord for my safety. Please give my kind regards to all my friends.

I remain, your affectionate brother,

William

The Battle of Gettysburg (Pa) was fought July 1–3, 1863. The battle involved the largest number of casualties of the entire war Union 3,150 killed 14,531 wounded. Confederate 4,708 killed 12,693 wounded. This was a decisive victory for the North. Source: The Battle of Gettysburg, Wikipedia.

Camp near Fredericksburg, Aug. 16, 1863

Dear Sister,

I take this present opportunity to let you know that I am well and hope these few lines may find you the same. I have just received your welcome letter dated June 21. I was truly glad to hear that you were enjoying good health and hope you will continue so. I am very sorry to hear of the misfortune that happened to Mrs. Muller's little daughter. I hope she may soon recover. We have just returned from our campaign into Pennsylvania. It was an active one. We met the Yankees at Gettysburg, Pa., where they were strongly fortified. We attacked them in their strong position but could not succeed in dislodging them and consequently had to fall back. The fight lasted 3 days and was one of the severest ever fought during this war. Our loss was very heavy. That of the enemy was still larger. A great many of our wounded were left in Pa., among them was Charley Settle. He was wounded in the shoulder. Ham has since received a letter from him stating that he was in Washington and was getting along very well. Ham is well and sends his kind regards to you. The following is a list of the killed and wounded in our company: killed,

W.H. Porter, J.W. Southwick, J. Waters. Th. Mellhausen. Wounded, J. Brown in leg, W. Taylor in arm, J. Cummings in leg, H. McGan in hand, A.M. Farquer in face, W. Shepperd in hand, A. Wood in leg. Several of those wounded are well and now with the company. Henry Truehart has been to see us a few days ago. He looks well. He says he is going to join Stuart's cavalry. He wants to see service.

Dear Sister, it is very difficult to get letters across the Mississippi River since the fall of Vicksburg. I will try and send this by hand. Everything is quiet along here. I do not think we will have any fight here soon. I am well and thanks be to the Lord for my safety. Fruit is plentiful here, but watermelons sell ten dollars apiece and very small at that. The sun is hot and I will have to go on drill in a few minutes.

Please give my kind regards to all my friends.

Your affectionate brother,

William

P.S. Les Thompson is in camp and doing well and sends his kind regards to you all.

The next letter seems to refer to the battle of Chickamauga, Sept. 19 – 20, 1863. The battle was second only to Gettysburg in the number of casualties and was a resounding defeat for the Union forces. The battle took place in Southeastern Tennessee and Northwestern Georgia.

Madison, Georgia, Oct. 26, 1863

Dear Sister,

I take this present opportunity to let you know how I am getting along. The last letter which I received from you was dated in June. I was very glad to hear that you were well. I will try and send this letter by politeness of Major Dunnwoody, who is here on business for the government and will return to Texas in a few days. Since my last letter there has been quite a change in military affairs. Longstreet's corps which we belong to, has been transferred from General Lee's army to Genl. Bragg's army in Tennessee. We left Port Royal, Va., on the 7 of Sept. and arrived at Bragg's army on the 18 of Sept., just one day before the big fight. Next day we began skirmishing with the enemy until 3 o'clock, when a heavy battle ensued in which I was wounded. A minie went in my knee and struck the bone and glanced off. The battle lasted two days and ended in the routing of the enemy and driving him into his entrenchments in Chattanooga, where he now remains. We captured six thousand prisoners and 60 pieces of artillery. The loss of my company was severe. The following is a list of casualties: Jack Lewis killed, B. C. Crawford died of his wounds, C.H. Kingsley wounded in the arm, J. Pratt in leg, A. Kelso in both legs, J. Murphy in the foot, Wm.

Leach in leg, P. Gilles in hand, A. Wood in leg, Wm.
Sheppard in foot, James Nagle in face, A. Brandt in face,
D. Elmendorf in foot, F. Schmidt in arm, J. Fralish in
arm, Lieut. R.A. Armstrong in arm, Lieut. W.P. Randall
taken prisoner, J. Coffey missing, Wm. Robinson in the
shoulder, S. Lazarus in leg, Wm. Schadt in leg, B.C.
Crawford was wounded with a piece of shell, he died
six days after the fight. Myself and his brother were
with him when he died. His loss will be a severe one to
his parents. He was one of my mess mates ever since we
left Galveston and I regret his loss deeply. Dear Sister, I
am now at the house of Col. J.B. Walker in Madison, Ga.
Mr. Walker is a very kind and wealthy gentleman. He
owns two plantations in Texas and two here. He came
to the hospital and took me and several other Texans to
his house and says he wants us to stay with him until
we get perfectly well. My wound is doing very well and
I will be able to join my company in a few weeks. Les
Thompson was struck with a piece of spent shell but
did not break the skin. He was well when last I saw
him. Ham Settle was well and not wounded in the last
fight. Charley Settle is well and still a prisoner. He was
not wounded so some exchanged prisoners report.
George Robbens was wounded and doing well when
last heard of. General Hood lost his leg in the last fight.
Genl Jenkins is in command in his place.

Dear Sister, I cannot speak in too high a term of Mr. and
Mrs. Walker for their kindness towards me. Mr. Walker
is well acquainted in Galveston. He is the father-in-law
of W.H. Goddard. I am having quite a fine time and
know how to appreciate it just about this time. My

wound was very painful, but thank the Lord I am all right now.

I remain, your affectionate brother,
William

A.J. Scott of my company was killed by falling off the cars.

I believe Col. J. B. Walker is John Byne Walker, Sr. (1805 – 1884) of Madison, Georgia. He owned a large amount of land in Georgia and Texas and was also involved in the expanding railroads of the day. I can only assume that this large house with slaves would have seemed luxurious to William. Source: Geni and Wikipedia article Bonar Hall.

Madison, Ga., Nov. 14, 1863

Dear Sister,

I now take my pen in hand to let you know that I am well and hope you enjoy the same blessing. I am still at the house of Mrs. Walker. My wound is well entirely and I will start for my regiment in a few days. Mrs. Walker has provided me with plenty of under clothes and socks. May the Lord bless her for her kindness. Mr. Walker had two sons in the army. One of them was wounded at Gettysburg and has since died. This is the first time that I have been away from my command and the first time that I have ever had a chance to witness and appreciate the feelings of the citizens of old Georgia, and I find them very kind and clever, and especially the young ladies.

I have just received a letter from Chas. Kingsley from my company. He was wounded in the battle of Chickamauga and has now lost the use of his arm. He has got a furlough. He says he is going to make his way to Texas. If he does I will send a letter by him. You may possibly get to see him, for he will go either to Galveston or Houston.

I have not heard a word from the Settle boys since I have been wounded. I am anxiously looking for a letter from you. Please write soon. A great many of the wounded boys have returned to the regiment. I will be there in a few days. Please give my kind regards to all my friends.

I remain, your affectionate brother,

William

Loudon, Tenn., Nov 22, 1863

Dear Sister,

I drop you these few lines to let you know that I am
well and I hope you enjoy the same blessings. I am now
on my way to my regiment. I expected to find it at
Loudon, but on arriving here I find that they have gone
to Knoxville, which is thirty miles from this place. Genl.
Longstreet and his corps have been sent to east
Tennessee to clean out Burnside. I hope we will
succeed. Burnside and his army are now in Knoxville
and our troops are within a mile of the town. Continual
skirmishing is going on and we expect to fight daily. I
am here with Capt. Baldwin and I am awaiting an
opportunity to get a ride in one of the wagons to the
regiment as I am not able to march as yet. My wound is
healed but I have not gotten the entire use of my leg as
yet. I intend to stay with the regiment while in camp
and when on a march I will go with the wagons until I
get all right. I am glad to say that I had quite a fine time
during my stay at Col. J.B. Walker's in Madison, Ga. I
was treated just as if I had been their own son and I
shall ever remember them for their kindness. There is
some talk here now about the Texas Brigade being
furloughed next spring to go to Texas. I hope it is true. I
will send this letter by Jas. Nagle who is going home on
furlough. Les Thompson is well and with the company.
I have not heard from the Settle boys lately. Please give
my kind regards to all my friends. Write soon. In haste.

I remain, your affectionate brother,
William

Camp near Bulls Gap, Tenn.
March 15, 1864

Dear Sister,

Your welcome letter dated Jan. 17 has just come to hand and I am glad to hear that you are well. I am well and hearty and hope these few lines may find you the same. Every thing is quiet here at present as far as military affairs are concerned. Genl. Longstreet's men have all reenlisted. I expect we will go into Kentucky this spring. The campaign has opened in our favor so far and I hope it will continue so. We have heard several reports about the Yankees having possession of Galveston and Sabine, but I do not believe it. I do not think that the Yankees will ever get into the interior of Texas. We are perfectly ignorant of what is going on in Texas, as we receive no papers at all, but I suppose it is all right. Hope so any way. Frank Gearing has just arrived here and has joined our company. He was captured while running the blockade. He has been exchanged. Ham and Les are both well and send their kind regards. Charley Settle is expected here every day as they have again agreed upon an exchange. It is reported that Genl. Morgan is going to join Genl. Longstreet on his raid into Kentucky. If it is true he will surely make those Yankees suffer for his imprisonment in the penitentiary. He now commands a large cavalry force. He is a worthy commander. I must come to a close. Please excuse this short letter in haste. Give kind regards to all my friends. Write soon.

I remain, your most affectionate brother,

William

The Battle of the Wilderness was fought in Spotsylvania County, just 50 miles north of Richmond. There are varying estimates of casualties with around 17 – 18,000 for the union and 10 – 12,000 for the confederate. Following the battle and in spite of the large losses the Union army remained on the offensive. Source: Battle of the Wilderness Wikipedia. The previous battle William refers to may have been the Battle Of Walkerton, A failed raid on Richmond lead by Col. Ulric Dahlgren. Papers found on Dahlgren's body contained an order to burn Richmond and assassinate Lee and his Cabinet. This news could have been expected to reach Caroline in Texas.

Lynchburg, May 25, 1864

Dear Sister,

I take this present opportunity to let you know how I am getting along. I was wounded in the right side at the Battle of the Wilderness fought on the 6th day of May. I remained at the field hospital for 16 days after I was wounded. I just arrived at this place yesterday and am now staying at the College Hospital at this place. My wound is not dangerous, although very painful. It is healing very fast and if nothing happens to me I will be with my company in a few weeks. The battle was a very severe one. Our loss is heavy, but that of the enemy is still greater. Their loss is estimated at 45 thousand according to their own papers. A great many of their dead are still unburied. Both armies are now near Hanover Junction, which is 25 miles from Richmond. Another battle is expected daily. General Grant says he is going to take Richmond in 40 days, but I suppose we will have something to say about that. He will find

Richmond a hard road to travel. I am in good health and spirits and hope these few lines will find you the same. I suppose you have heard the particulars about the battle before this. You must excuse me for not writing sooner for this is the only chance I have had since I have been wounded. The following is a list of casualties in the company: killed, Lieut. W. P. Randall, Private G. Baker and Fred Cole. Wounded, Capt. W. Beddel in the side, Lieut. R. Armstrong in the hip, F. Schmidt lost the left arm, F. Gearing in the shoulder, John McCarty in the shoulder, J. Welch in the hip, Peter Gilles in the arm, J. Fralish in the arm, C.L. Bolling in the leg, H. Shultz in the leg, Les Thompson in the arm. Missing, C.H. Kingsley, S.D. Sims, O.A. Brandt. The missing are supposed to be taken prisoners. Ham Settle was all right when last I heard from him, which was after the battle. Charley had not arrived up to that time, but was expected every day, but I suppose this fighting has interfered with the flag of truce arrangements. Les Thompson was wounded very slightly and I expect he has returned to the company. The wounded are all doing very well. I don't like a hospital and will be very glad when I get able to leave it, which I hope is very soon.

I have survived another great battle without great injury and I am very thankful to Providence for my narrow escape. Please give my kind regards to all my friends. Write soon. I am anxious to hear from you. So no more at present.

Your affectionate brother,

William

Camp near Petersburg, July 23, 1864

Dear Sister,

I have just received your welcome letter dated May the 1st. I was truly glad to hear that you were well. I have also received a letter from Eugene dated June 8. Please tell Eugene that I am under many obligations to him for his kindness. Dear Sister, it is with deep regret that I inform you of the death of our dear friend, Hamilton Settle, who was wounded on the 14th of July in the neck and has since died in Richmond. Charley Settle has made his escape from Fort Delaware and arrived in Richmond on the same day that his brother was buried. How sad it is to think that this world is nothing but a tide of troubles. Poor Ham, he has left this land of troubles and gone to the Kingdom of Heaven, which is prepared for those who hear and obey the laws of God. I am proud to say that he was both a true and faithful Christian and a soldier. Charley has got a furlough, but I do not know where he is going. I hope it is to Texas. He is well and hearty.

Dear Sister, I have just recovered from a wound received in my right side at the Battle of the Wilderness, fought on the 6th day of May. My wound was very painful, but I am willing to bear all such if I do not receive any worse. I am at present in good health and spirits and hope you are the same. We are in the entrenchments about two miles from town. The Yankees are also in entrenchments four hundred yards from us. Cannonading and picket firing is kept up pretty regular day and night. I do not think that the enemy will attempt to storm our works, but will try to flank us, but at any rate we are ready to play him any time he chooses. General Early commanding Ewell's old corps, has made a raid into Maryland, and has captured a large amount of stores, horses, mules, cattle, etc., and has returned safe to Virginia with all his plunder. He has also done great damage to the railroads. General Johnston has been relieved from his command and General Hood has taken his place. If General Hood losses any ground it will not be by retreating, but by hard fighting, for such he is used to, for I know that by experience. Eugene wishes my opinion about this war. Tell him I think that there will be a great change this fall or winter, and besides I think we shall see peace before twelve months. Jas. Nagle has not arrived yet.

Dear Sister, I am very glad to hear that you have met with such friends. I would very much like to see them. I did not get that ring you spoke of. I do not know anything about George Robins, last that I saw of him was at the field hospital at Chickamauga. He was then wounded in the arm and doing well. Les Thompson is a clerk at a hospital near this place and doing well. Please tell Billy Young to write me and tell me what has become of all my old friends. Please give my kind regards to all my friends and acquaintances. Write soon. No more at present. In haste. Please excuse bad writing, shells are flying.

With much love, your affectionate brother, William

Near Chaffin's Bluff, Sept. 15, 1864

My dear Sister,

I have just received your kind letter dated July the 23rd. I am glad to hear that you are enjoying good health and hope you may continue so. I am in good health and hope you are the same. We are at present in line of battle near Chaffin's Bluff where we have been for the last four weeks. Everything is quiet along here except cannonading which is kept up from Chaffin's Bluff to Petersburg, sometimes day and night. Artillery duel and picket fighting is a daily occurrence and have long since ceased to create excitement. You speak in your letter about me trying to get a furlough. I tried my best but did not succeed, but I may have a chance to get one this winter and if so I will be sure to come home. I will try to send this by hand as a Lieut. in the 5th is going to Houston. Joseph and James Nagle are both in Richmond. I received the socks which you sent by Joe. I am very thankful to you for them. James Nagle will return to Texas next month. Chas. Settle has just returned from his furlough. He is well and sends his kind regards. George Robins is in Richmond. He is trying to get his retired papers and if he succeeds he will go to Texas. He has lost the use of his arm, otherwise he is well and hearty. Les Thompson is sick with fever but is now getting better. He had quite a hard time. Fred Delesdenier is well and sends his kind regards. Please give my kind regards to all my friends. No more at present.

Your affectionate brother,

William

F. Les Thompson is one of the people William has been reporting on throughout his letters, but I am left to wonder about the informality of his address of Caroline. In the last letter of the collection Caroline returns the informality by referriung to him as Les, while referring to everyone else as Mr., Mrs., or with first and last name.

> In line of battle, Darbytown
> Road, near Richmond, Va.
> Oct. 14, 1864

Miss Lina Schadt
Houston

It is a painful duty that impels me to write to you. Prepare yourself to hear bad news. I will no longer keep you in suspense, but write the whole truth at once. Your brother, William, on the 7 of Oct. was wounded (but not seriously), and left in the enemy's hands. We were charging a Yankee fort when he was struck, and being repulsed, had to fall back, leaving most our badly wounded on the field. William, I am certain, was not very seriously injured. Shot probably in the leg. Do not fear, Lina, he will be well taken care of. Trust in God, and pray daily for your captured brother. As soon as we hear from him we will write again. My God grant you strength and fortitude to bear up under this calamity. Say with Christ in the garden "Thy will be done, oh God."

> Yours truly,
>
> F. Les Thompson

Richmond, Va.
Jan. 13, 1865

Dear Miss Schadt,

Presuming you have heard the report ere this of the
death of your brother, William, I hasten to write to you
to contradict the report, having heard from him last
night. I am happy to say Billy is safe (only a prisoner). I
know your great anxiety for him and I write you
accordingly. I am at present wounded in Howard Grace
Hospital. Billy was a good and true friend of mind, and
I feel much interest in him and his reputation is
untarnished as a man and soldier.

I am very respectfully,

A. Wakelee
Co. L, 1st Texas Regt.
Greggs Brigade

The Point Lookout camp was located in St. Mary's County, Maryland. The Prisoner of war camp was built to house 10,000 prisoners, but at times held as many as 20,000. It was consider one of the worse northern camps. The location is preserve as the Point Lookout State Park. Source: Point Lookout State Park, Wikipedia.

Richmond, Va., Feb. 26, 1865

My dear Sister,

I have just arrived here from Point Lookout where I have been a prisoner of war for nearly five months. I was slightly wounded and captured on the 7 day of Oct. I am not exchanged as yet. I am expecting to get a furlough and I will try to go to Texas if it is possible. George Branard is going to Texas this evening. I will send this note by him. I have just received your letter dated Oct. 15, which was the first I heard from you since my capture. I was glad to hear that you were well. I will write you a letter tomorrow. I am in good health and doing well. You must excuse this bad writing. I am in haste. I will tell you all particulars tomorrow. Give my kind regards to all.

Yours,

William Schadt

Houston, March 29, 1865

My ever dear Brother,

I came to Houston on a visit for a few days, looking all the while for a letter from you, and was made happy by receiving a letter from your friend, Mr. Wakelee, saying he had heard from you and you were safe. I say happy – yes, happy if I can be happy without my darling Willie. God will bless Mr. Wakelee for his kindness in writing to me. I hear you were wounded. Write and tell me all about it. I hope you are in good health and spirits. Trust in God, He knows what is best for us. Mr. Wakelee did not say what prison you were in, but I hope this will reach you to let you know that I am well.

I have been to see Mr. Gearing. He speaks in the highest terms of you. He says you are one of the noblest boys in the world. He will take your socks on for me if he can send them to you he will, I am sure, for he thinks so much of you. Mrs. Crane and family are all well. Miss Ellen Settle is up here. She wants me to go home with her, but I am not ready to go yet. Mr. and Mrs. Santers are well. All send much love. I had a letter from Les but he did not know where you were. I have written you before. All your friends here are well. Brother dear, if the prayers of a loving and affectionate sister are answered you will come home safe.

My kind regards to your friends, if you have any there. If I can write let me know and I will write often.

With much love, your affectionate sister,

Caroline

God bless and keep you from harm and let you return home safe.

The War ended with surrender at Appomattox on April 9, 1865. Perhaps William still had this final letter from Caroline with him when he arrived home.

Epilogue

After the war, Caroline (Lina) continued to live with the Cranes. Mr. Crane's sister, Ella Theodocia was married to John Ansell and lived in Rhinebeck New York. Their son, Walter Crane Ansell came to Galveston in 1858. When he went to visit his uncle, Caroline Schadt either held his horse for him or served him lemonade. Walter thought it was terrible the way the Cranes were treating this "delicate girl" as a servant. Walter worked with steamboats between Houston and Galveston. In 1871 he settled in Galveston where he was listed as Secretary and Treasurer for The Texas Ice Company. Walter Crane Ansell and Caroline Schaefer Schadt were married June 21, 1871, in the Crane's home. They had three children; Ella Theodocia Ansell Fraser 1872 - 1956, John William Ansell 1874 – 1928, and Wallace Schadt Ansell 1881 - 1939. Walter died on December 21, 1911. Caroline died August 17, 1909.

Following the war, William lived with the Cranes and later with his sister and her new husband. William met his future wife Emma Ida Keller while she was working as a maid for the Cranes. They were married February 9, 1885, at Grace Episcopal Church in Galveston. In 1888 William bought the W. F. Stewart & Co. a hardware store he renamed it WM. SCHADT "The Building Supply House." It was located at 28th and Mechanic. They had eight children all who lived into adulthood. Charles Ansell 1885 – 1969, Lilian 1888 – 1978, Myrtle Mae 1890 – 1983, Ewald Keller 1892 – 1947, William

Frederick, Jr. 1894 – 1933, Ida Vivian 1897 – 1891, Everett Walter 1901 -1991, and Louis Grey 1903 – 1901,. Charles was my Grandfather. William died in 1917. The store burned before William's death and was relocated to the Strand. After William's death, the store was run by his sons Louis and Charles and later by a manager. The store was again damaged when a hurricane made landfall on the Bolivar Peninsula, July of 1943. In 1956 or 57 the store was sold to Mr. Niederman, who continued in business as Niedermann – Schadt, Housewares, and Hardware.

As a six-year-old I can remember being taken to the bedside of my Great Grandmother Schadt and I remember being taken out of school to attend her funeral. She was 102.

Stuart E. Schadt Editor

Cover Photo
Inscription
The Texas Civil War Monument
Manassas National Battlefield Park

ERECTED BY THE STATE OF TEXAS 2012

Texas

REMEMBERS THE VALOR AND DEVOTION OF HER SOLDIERS WHO PARTICIPATED IN THE BATTLE OF SECOND MANASSAS, VIRGINIA--AUGUST 28-30, 1862.

ON THIS FIELD, CONFEDERATE GEN. ROBERT E. LEE'S ARMY OF NORTHERN VIRGINIA WON THE DECISIVE BATTLE OF THE NORTHERN VIRGINIA CAMPAIGN, AGAINST UNION MAJ. GEN. JOHN POPE'S ARMY OF VIRGINIA. ARRIVING ON THE SECOND DAY AUGUST 29TH, CONFEDERATE MAJ. GEN. JAMES LONGSTREET'S WING TOOK POSITION OPPOSITE POPE'S LEFT FLANK. LATE THAT AFTERNOON BRIG. GEN. JOHN BELL HOOD'S TEXAS BRIGADE SAW ITS FIRST COMBAT OF THE ENGAGEMENT, ADVANCING INTO THE UNION LINE. AT GROVETON, THEIR POSITION UNTENABLE, THE BRIGADE WITHDREW THE FOLLOWING MORNING. MISINTERPRETING CONFEDERATE MANEUVERS AS A RETREAT, GEN. POPE ORDERED ANOTHER ATTACK ON GEN. STONEWALL JACKSON'S POSITION ON AUGUST 30TH. WITH THE HELP OF GEN. LONGSTREET'S ARTILLERY, THE UNION ATTACK WAS REPULSED. GEN. LONGSTREET'S FIVE DIVISIONS THEN COUNTERATTACKED IN ONE OF THE LARGEST, SIMULTANEOUS MASS ASSAULTS OF THE WAR. HOOD'S TEXAS BRIGADE LED THE ADVANCE WITH THE ENTIRE WING PIVOTING ON THE BRIGADE. IN THE ENSUING COMBAT HOOD'S TEXAS BRIGADE OVERWHELMED THE 5TH AND 10TH NEW YORK ZOUAVES AT GROVETON AND DROVE OFF A BRIGADE OF PENNSYLVANIA RESERVES. THEIR EFFORTS CLIMAXED WITH THE CAPTURE OF KERN'S PENNSYLVANIA BATTERY. ALTHOUGH THE TERRAIN AND STUBBORN UNION RESISTANCE ON CHINN RIDGE ULTIMATELY BROKE THE TACTICAL INTEGRITY OF THE UNIT, THE TEXAS BRIGADE CONTRIBUTED SIGNIFICANTLY TO THE COLLAPSE OF THE UNION LEFT FLANK WHICH FORCED POPE'S RETREAT THAT NIGHT AND OPENED THE WAY FOR LEE'S INVASION OF MARYLAND.

*Back panel inscription, Texas Civil War Monument, Second
Manassas, Virginia:*

TEXAS UNITS ENGAGED IN
THE BATTLE OF SECOND MANASSAS, VA.

BRIG. GEN. JOHN BELL HOOD'S BRIGADE

1ST TEXAS
VOLUNTEER INFANTRY REGIMENT

4TH TEXAS
VOLUNTEER INFANTRY REGIMENT

5TH TEXAS
VOLUNTEER INFANTRY REGIMENT

18TH GEORGIA
VOLUNTEER INFANTRY REGIMENT

HAMPTON'S LEGION, SOUTH CAROLINA
(8 INFANTRY COMPANIES)

TEXAS UNITS FORMED THE MAJOR PORTION OF
HOOD'S BRIGADE, THUS IT WAS COMMONLY KNOWN
AS THE TEXAS BRIGADE. BUT THE 18TH GEORGIA,
HAMPTON'S LEGION, AND LATER THE 3RD ARKANSAS
WERE INTEGRAL PARTS OF THE BRIGADE.

TEXAS REMEMBERS AND HONORS HER SONS
AND THOSE OF HER SISTER STATES WHO
FOUGHT WITH THEM.
THEY SLEEP THE SLEEP OF THE BRAVE.

INDEX

1st Texas Volunteer Infantry Regiment
Company L – Lone Star Rifles

McKEEN, ALFRED C. Capt. –
BEDELL, WM. A. 1Lt.
THOMPSON, J. C. S. 2Lt.
BALDWIN, JOHN M. 3Lt.

ORIGINAL NON-COMMISSIONED OFFICERS
SMITH, ANDREW W. lSgt.
ARMSTRONG, ROET. R. 2Sgt
RICHARDSON, W. F. 3Sgt.
ROBINSON, W. B. 4Sgt.
FORSYTHE, A. P. lCpl.
RANDALL, W. P. 2Cpl.
ROBINSON, R. S. 3Cpl.
BRANARD, GEO. A. 4Cpl.

OTHER OFFICERS
VIDOR, CHAS. Capt.
ARMSTRONG, ROBT. R. iLt.
BOLLING, CHAS. L. 2Lt.
RANDALL, W. P. 2Lt.
FORSYTHE, A. P. 3Lt.

PRIVATES
ALSBROOK, JOS.
ATHERON, W. R.
BAKER, G. B.
BARBEE, WILSON J
BERNARD, THOS.
BLESSING, SAMUEL T.
BOLLING, CHAS. L.

BOSS (or BASS), GEO. - K.
BOURKE, DANIEL
BOURKE, JOHN
BOYKAIN (or BOYKIN), W. T.
BRANDT, A.
BROWN, JOHN W
BROWN, JOS. F.
BUCKLEY, EDWARD C.
CADY, D. C.
CARNES, WM. C
CARPENTER, STEPHEN A.
CARTER, G. W. L
CLARK, SAMUEL
COFFEE, JOHN – W.
COHEN, HENRY - W.
COLE, FRED T.
COLLINS, MONROE P.
CRAWFORD, B. C.
CUMMINGS, JAS. W.
CURTIS, R. A.
DAVIS, JOHN
DELESDENIER, L. F.
DILLON, JOHN
ELMENDORF, DAVID
FARQUAR, ADRIAN M.
FRALICH (or FRALISH), JOHN
FRANK, JACOB
GADIFFET, GUSTAV
GARITY (or GARRITY), MICHAEL
GEARING, F. A. G.
GILLIS, JOHN P.
HAGAN, CHAS.
HALLECK, CHAS. B.
HANSON, JOHN
HARRIS, JOHN
HAWKINS, GEO. B.

HOSKINS, WM.
HOYLE, CHAS. W.
JACKSON, WM. L
JACOBLEF, ROBT.
JONES, AUSTIN W.
KELSO, AARON
KIERAN, L.
KINGSLEY, CHAS. H.
LAKE, THOS. W. C.
LAZARUS, SALEM S.
LEACH, WM
LEWIS, JOHN
LOVELOCK, WM. H..
MAHONEY, J. P.
McCARTY, CHAS. W. .
McCARTY, JOHN M. .
McCARTY, THOS. L.
McCORQUODALE, EPHRAM A. .
McGAN, HENRY B..
MERK (or MERKE), GEO. A.
MEYERS, HENRY
MILLARD, WATSON C.
MELLHAUSEN, THEO. H.
MURPHY, J. W.
NAGLE, JAS.
NAGLE, JOS.
NELSON, JOHN
NICHOLS, FRANKLIN C.
NICHOLSON, JOHN B.
NOEL, BENJAMIN C.
PICKETT, JONATHAN
PORTER, WM. H.
POUPART, JOHN
PRATER, VIRGIL
PRATT (or PRUETT), JAS. C.
ROBINSON, WALTER M.

ROGERS, GEO.
ROOKS, NOAH
ROURKE, JOHN 0.
SABLE, JACK
SCHADT, CHAS.
SCHADT, WM.
SCHMIDT, FRANK
SCHULTZ, HENRY
SCHULTZ, HENRY P.
SCHWARTING, FRED
SCOTT, ALEXANDER J.
SCOTT, GEO. WASHINGTON
SHELTON, W. A.
SHEPHERD, W. G.
SIMMS, SMITH D.
SMITH, FRANK
SMITH, JOHN
SMITH, JOHN M. - W.
SMITH, SIDNEY B. - W.
SOLOMON, NATHANIEL B.
SOUTHWICK, J. W.
STANSBURY, N.J.
STARK, W. JASPER
STODDARD, BENNETT R.
TAYLOR, RICHARD H.
TAYLOR, WALLACE
THOMPSON, F. LESLIE
THOMPSON, LESLIE A.
TOWNSEND, J. L.
VARNELL, F. W.
VON HUTTON, WM. B.
WAGNER, M. L.
WAKELEE, AUGUSTUS
WATERS, JOHN D.
WELCH, JAS.
WILLIAMS, CHAS.

WOOD, ALBERT W.
WORSHAM, CHAS. S.
WORSHAM, JAS. N.
YOUNG, WM.
ZIMMER, WM.

Source: texas-brigade.org/1st_tex/1texrostercol.htm